GRAPHIC SCIENCE

THE EXPLOSIVE WORLD OF

VOLCANOES

WITH MAX AXIOM
SUPER SCIENTIST

by Christopher L. Harbo

illustrated by Tod Smith

Consultant:
Professor Kenneth H. Rubin
Department of Geology and Geophysics
School of Ocean and Earth Science and Technology
University of Hawaii, Honolulu

Capstone

Mankato, Minnesota

Graphic Library is published by Capstone Press,
151 Good Counsel Drive, P.O. Box 669, Mankato, Minnesota 56002.
www.capstonepress.com

Printed in the United States of America

1 2 3 4 5 6 12 11 10 09 08 07

Library of Congress Cataloging-in-Publication Data
Harbo, Christopher L.
The explosive world of volcanoes with Max Axiom, super scientist / by Christopher L.
Harbo; illustrated by Tod Smith.
p. cm.—(Graphic library. Graphic science)
Summary: "In graphic novel format, follows the adventures of Max Axiom as he
explains the science behind volcanoes"—Provided by publisher.
Includes bibliographical references and index.
ISBN-13: 978-1-4296-0144-3 (hardcover)
ISBN-10: 1-4296-0144-2 (hardcover)
1. Volcanoes—Juvenile literature. I. Smith, Tod, ill. II. Title. III. Series.
QE521.3.H24 2008
551.21—dc22   2006102361

Art Director
Bob Lentz

Designers
Thomas Emery and Kyle Grenz

Colorist
Matt Webb

Editors
Donald B. Lemke and Christine Peterson

The author dedicates this book to Ingrid, Torin, and Anja.

TABLE OF CONTENTS

Super Scientist Max Axiom begins his exploration of volcanoes on the slopes of Arenal in Costa Rica.

One more temperature reading should do the trick.

Just as I thought. This lava is hot enough to melt glass.

4

Volcanoes are fascinating structures. Arenal, here in Costa Rica, is no exception.

With nearly constant eruptions since 1968, Arenal is one of earth's most active volcanoes.

But not all volcanoes are towering cones that look and behave like Arenal.

In fact, a volcano is any hole in the ground that allows lava to rise up to the earth's surface.

While some volcanoes are cone-shaped, others are broad and flat.

And lava isn't the only material volcanoes spew. Hot gases, clouds of ash, and huge boulders sometimes shoot out of these amazing formations.

What brings you out to sea, Max?
The science of volcanoes, Dr. Flint. I understand you've been doing research on how volcanoes form.

That's right, Max. How volcanoes form depends on the way huge sections of the earth's crust move.
You're talking about earth's tectonic plates.
TECTONIC PLATES
Yes. These enormous sections of crust divide up our planet like a giant jigsaw puzzle.

Earth's plates are huge, but they don't always stay still.

Plate movement sometimes allows hot magma to rise to the surface through cracks in the crust.

As a result, most volcanoes form along plate boundaries where plates either pull apart or come together.

The Pacific Ocean has so many volcanoes along plate borders that this area is called the Ring of Fire.

Hot Spots

Not all volcanoes form on plate boundaries. Some form when magma pushes its way through the middle of a tectonic plate. These areas are called hot spots. The Hawaiian Islands formed above a hot spot in the middle of the Pacific Plate.

We're passing over a line of volcanoes forming on the ocean floor right now.

Would you like to take the mini-sub down for a look?

You bet!

With 70 percent of earth covered by water, most volcanoes are hidden deep under the oceans.
But the deepest, darkest place on earth gives us stunning views of newly forming volcanoes.
For instance, here we see how all volcanoes begin with a main vent.
This pipeline to the magma chamber allows hot gases and magma to travel from miles under the crust.

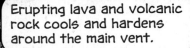

Erupting lava and volcanic rock cools and hardens around the main vent.

Over time, layers of material build up and form a circular crater around the vent.

Volcanoes can erupt for millions of years.

As the crater grows, volcanic material can erupt off to the side.

Side vents often branch off from the main vent, releasing steam, hot gases, and lava.

In that time, some underwater volcanoes add enough layers to break the surface.

When they do, islands form.

The earth has thousands of volcanoes, but few of them are active.

So, what is an active volcano?

In any given year, 50 to 70 volcanoes erupt around the world.

But erupting volcanoes are not the only ones considered active. Scientists consider any volcano that has erupted in the last few years to be active. Active volcanoes also show signs of molten magma beneath them.

By this measure, earth has about 550 active volcanoes.

Of course, most active and inactive volcanoes sit quietly year after year.

Scientists often label these sleeping giants as either dormant or extinct.

A dormant volcano is capable of erupting, but hasn't for many years.

An extinct volcano hasn't erupted in many thousands of years and isn't expected to erupt again.

Japan's Mount Fuji is a dormant volcano that hasn't erupted since 1708.

Hawaii's Kohala volcano hasn't erupted for 60,000 years. At this time, scientists believe it's extinct.

Of course, no one knows for sure when a dormant volcano may erupt or if an extinct volcano is really extinct.

Sleeping giants sometimes wake up.

Hot gases in magma shattered some of the rock into billions of tiny pieces. These pieces formed ash.

Larger rocks and boulders, called volcanic blocks, were flung from the volcano.

Mixed together, the searing gases, ash, and cinders created a pyroclastic flow. This deadly cloud raced down the volcano and flattened everything in its path.

Mount St. Helens' pyroclastic flow destroyed almost 150 square miles of forest. That's about 389 square kilometers.

It killed thousands of animals and 57 people near the volcano.

⚡ MUD SLIDES

A mud slide is one of the biggest dangers of a volcanic eruption. Mud slides form when pyroclastic flows melt snow near the top of a volcano. This flow also forms when heavy rains sweep huge amounts of steaming rock, debris, and water down the side of a volcano.

Of course, volcanic eruptions are most famous for spewing red-hot lava.

Let's visit a scientist who spends her days studying lava from Hawaii's Kilauea volcano.

Kilauea is putting on quite a show, Dr. Maka.

Yes, Kilauea has produced a lot of lava for me to study since this eruption began in 1983.

In fact, the rock we're standing on is made of lava. After it flowed down from Kilauea's vent, the lava cooled and hardened.

This fresh lava must be one of the two types of lava flows that have Hawaiian names.

That's right. This lava flow is known as pahoehoe.

"Pa-hoy-hoy." That's fun to say.

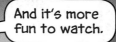

But here on the volcanic island of Iceland, some of the volcanoes have a very different look.

Iceland has many cinder cone volcanoes.

Cinder cones are usually smaller and much steeper than shield volcanoes. They form when globs of lava are thrown into the air by an eruption.

As the lava globs fall, they break apart and cool into cinders that pile up around the volcano's central vent.

The third type of volcano is probably the easiest to identify.

Popocatepetl, or El Popo, in Mexico is a super example of a stratovolcano.

Stratovolcanoes are tall, towering cones. They form as layer upon layer of lava and ash build up over time.

CRATER

SUBJECT:
STRATOVOLCANO
POPOCATEPETL

NEW LAVA FLOW

OLD LAVA FLOW

El Popo's layers have built up over thousands of years. Today, the volcano's cone rises about 17,800 feet or 5,425 meters above sea level.

X-RAY ENABLED

As we've seen, the material erupted has a lot to do with how a volcano looks.

But sometimes eruptions are so violent they tear volcanoes down.

Welcome to Wyoming's Yellowstone National Park. It's one of the most active calderas in the world.

The Yellowstone region is made up of three overlapping calderas. These calderas formed during massive eruptions 2 million, 1.2 million, and 600,000 years ago.

A caldera is a volcano that lost its upper slopes when they collapsed into the magma chamber during an eruption.

Today, magma beneath Yellowstone's main caldera fuels spectacular geysers, hot springs, and mud pots.

Volcanoes are breathtaking to behold, but the world has seen many deadly eruptions.

Let's visit one of the most devastating eruptions of the 20th century. It happened on the French Caribbean Island of Martinique.

At the start of the 1900s, St. Pierre was known as the "Paris of the West Indies."

This busy harbor city was nestled at the base of Mount Pelée.

In early 1902, Mount Pelée began having a series of minor eruptions.

These eruptions alarmed people, but no one expected the tragedy that was about to unfold.

The city of Pompeii was lost for more than 1,600 years.

When it was finally rediscovered, people began learning about the terror Vesuvius had unleashed on the city in AD 79.

They found that the victims of the eruption had been encased in ash. Over time, that ash had hardened around the bodies.

The bodies had then decayed, but hollow spaces that matched the body shapes remained.

In the late 1800s, scientists invented a way to make plaster casts of the bodies in these hollow spaces.

Today, scientists study these casts to learn more about how the people of Pompeii died.

⚡ HERCULANEUM

Pompeii wasn't the only city destroyed by Mount Vesuvius' eruption in AD 79. Mud flows buried the city of Herculaneum under 65 feet (20 meters) of ash and rock.

At volcanoes around the world, these scientists measure the temperature of lava, take gas samples, and monitor changes in landforms.

By understanding volcanic behavior, they hope to predict future eruptions. Then scientists can warn people when current eruptions become hazardous to people living nearby.

Their jobs are dangerous, but the work they do is important.

Because you never know when we'll see the next big eruption.

Lava and pyroclastic flows often destroy everything in their paths. Ash and lava carry many nutrients plants need to grow. After many years, hard lava flows become the soil plants and trees thrive on.

Lava is super hot, but it's not the most dangerous thing a volcano erupts. Lava usually moves so slowly that people have time to get out of its way. Huge mud slides and heated clouds of ash and gases are much more dangerous for people living near an eruption.

In October 2004, Mount St. Helens began erupting again. Although the eruptions were minor, the new activity pushed a massive rock slab out of the crater's dome. For a time, the rock slab stood about the length of a football field out of the crater.

In 1991, the eruption of Mount Pinatubo in the Philippines affected the weather around the world. Ash carried worldwide in the air blocked out some sunlight. In the year after the eruption, temperatures around the globe fell an average of 1 degree.

Iceland is one of the few places people can see two of earth's plates spreading apart above sea level. Each year, the plates move apart about 1 inch (2.5 centimeters). As a result, Iceland has many active volcanoes, geysers, and hot springs.

Some scientists use space satellites to study volcanoes. Satellites measure heat released by a volcano and track eruption clouds as they travel around the globe.

Earth isn't the only place in our solar system where volcanoes have formed. Venus, Mars, and Jupiter's moon, Io, also have many volcanoes. In fact, Olympus Mons on Mars is the largest known volcano in the solar system. This huge shield volcano is about the size of the state of Arizona. It rises 15 miles (24 kilometers) above the surface of Mars.

Scientists use an electric thermometer to measure the temperature of lava. This thermometer is made of ceramic and stainless steel. These materials can stand up to lava's high temperatures.

MORE ABOUT

MAX AXIOM
SUPER SCIENTIST

Real name: Maxwell J. Axiom
Hometown: Seattle, Washington
Height: 6' 1"   Weight: 192 lbs
Eyes: Brown   Hair: None

Super capabilities: Super intelligence; able to shrink to the size of an atom; sunglasses give x-ray vision; lab coat allows for travel through time and space.

Origin: Since birth, Max Axiom seemed destined for greatness. His mother, a marine biologist, taught her son about the mysteries of the sea. His father, a nuclear physicist and volunteer park ranger, schooled Max on the wonders of earth and sky.

One day on a wilderness hike, a megacharged lightning bolt struck Max with blinding fury. When he awoke, Max discovered a newfound energy and set out to learn as much about science as possible. He traveled the globe earning degrees in every aspect of the field. Upon his return, he was ready to share his knowledge and new identity with the world. He had become Max Axiom, Super Scientist.

GLOSSARY

caldera (kal-DER-ah)—a collapsed volcano

cinder (SIN-dur)—a cooled piece of lava from an erupting volcano

cone (KOHN)—the tip of a volcano

crust (KRUHST)—the thin outer layer of Earth's surface

dormant (DOR-muhnt)—not active; dormant volcanoes have not erupted for many years.

erupt (e-RUHPT)—to suddenly burst; a volcano shoots steam, lava, and ash into the air when it erupts.

extinct (ek-STINGKT)—no longer active; a volcano is extinct if it has stopped erupting for thousands of years.

lava (LAH-vuh)—the hot, liquid rock that pours out of a volcano when it erupts

magma (MAG-muh)—melted rock found beneath the surface of Earth

mantle (MAN-tuhl)—the layer of super-hot rock that surrounds Earth's core

molten (MOHLT-uhn)—melted by heat; lava is molten rock.

plate (PLAYT)—a large sheet of rock that is a piece of Earth's crust

pyroclastic flow (peye-roh-KLAS-tik FLOH)—a moving mixture of hot gases, ash, and rock from a volcano; a pyroclastic flow can reach speeds of up to 100 miles (161 kilometers) per hour.

vent (VENT)—a hole in a volcano; hot ash, steam, and lava blow out of vents from an erupting volcano.

READ MORE

Armentrout, David, and Patricia Armentrout. *Volcanoes.* Earth's Power. Vero Beach, Fla: Rourke, 2007.

Colson, Mary. *Earth Erupts: Volcanoes.* Turbulent Planet. Chicago: Raintree, 2006.

Dayton, Connor. *Volcanic Rocks.* Rocks and Minerals. New York: PowerKids Press, 2007.

Green, Jen. *Mount St. Helens.* Disasters. Milwaukee: Gareth Stevens, 2005.

Kaplan, Sarah Pitt. *Pompeii.* Digging Up the Past. New York: Children's Press, 2005.

Stille, Darlene R. *Plate Tectonics: Earth's Moving Crust.* Exploring Science. Minneapolis: Compass Point Books, 2006.

INTERNET SITES

FactHound offers a safe, fun way to find Internet sites related to this book. All of the sites on FactHound have been researched by our staff.

Here's how:
1. Visit *www.facthound.com*
2. Choose your grade level.
3. Type in this book ID **1429601442** for age-appropriate sites. You may also browse subjects by clicking on letters, or by clicking on pictures and words.
4. Click on the **Fetch It** button.

FactHound will fetch the best sites for you!